Dedicated to the wonder in childhood,
the beauty of nature,
and Jenny.

E.L.Z. & J.T.

Text copyright 2006 by Eileen L. Ziesler
Illustrations copyright 2006 by Janelle Thompson
Photograph copyright 2007 by Peter Olson

First Edition 2008
Printed in China by Artful Dragon Press

oad House Publishing

USA

Book design by Eileen L. Ziesler and Janelle Thompson
The text of this book is set in Papyrus. The illustrations are water color reproduced in full color.

Summary: When day dawns, the toads hide.
We wonder where they can be and if they will come out again in the night.

Publisher's Cataloging-In-Publication Data

(Prepared by The Donohue Group, Inc.)

Ziesler, Eileen L.

    Toads : a poem / by Eileen L. Ziesler ; illustrated by Janelle Thompson. -- 1st ed.

  p. : col. ill. ; cm.

  Interest age level: 003-007.
  ISBN: 978-0-9818831-0-6

1. Toads--Juvenile poetry. 2. Children's poetry, American. 3. Toads--Poetry. 4. American poetry. I. Thompson, Janelle. II. Title.

PS3626.137 T63 2008

811/.6   2008905905

Toads

A Poem by Eileen L. Ziesler

Illustrated by Janelle L Thompson

Where do the toads
go in the morn

When the moon
goes down
and the sun

grows warm

When the damp of the dew,
cooling the night

Evaporates
into the hot sunlight?

Where do they hide?
Where can they be?

I search everywhere
but I cannot see.

Do they head for the beach
and the dry hot sand?

Will they slather on lotion
to avoid a suntan?

Do they make for the woods
and the soft cushy moss?

Will they snack on mosquitoes
and sip a dew wash?

Where do they hide?
Where can they be?

I search everywhere
but I cannot see.

The sun goes down
and the ground
grows damp.

Will they come out
in the light
of the lamp?

About the Author and Illustrator

Eileen L. Ziesler (author) worked toward her master's degree in special education between 1973 and 1977 while becoming a mother to three children. In 1978, Janelle Thompson (illustrator) was also a young mother with two little girls. When her oldest child, Jenny, did not follow the expected developmental trajectory, Janelle asked the school district to provide an early childhood program. Eileen became the program's first teacher and Jenny became her first student. As part of the early childhood program, Eileen made visits to Jenny's home where she and Jenny's mother became good friends.

Twenty-four years passed and Eileen retired from the early childhood program to other dreams of writing and community involvement. In those same years Janelle developed her talent for creating wildlife watercolors. Jenny grew up and gained employment in the community. Through a mentoring program in 2004, Jenny and Eileen found each other again and became friends. Because of Jenny, Eileen and Janelle renewed their friendship and collaborated on their first picture book, TOADS. Other picture books celebrating the wonder in childhood through the beauty of Janelle's artwork are in progress.

Jenny, Janelle, and Eileen

Photo by Peter Olson

About the Photographer

Peter Olson (photographer) enjoys outdoor sports and photography in nature. He formerly did black and white darkroom printing along with color photography. The digital boom revived his interest in making prints, and he now uses the computer and a photo printer instead of a chemical darkroom. Peter enjoys photographing landscapes, buildings, and portraits in northern Wisconsin.

About Toads (<u>bufonidae bufo</u>)

Toads are amphibians, the class of animals that spend their time as eggs and tadpoles underwater and the remainder of their lives on land. They are nocturnal hunters, catching insects and other small animals with long sticky tongues. They take shelter in cool locations during the day. You can find toads everywhere except the cold, polar regions of the world and Australia.

Most toads are warty fellows protected from becoming the main course of larger animals by the poison glands behind their eyes that emit a milky substance when they are caught. Toads are chubby with shorter legs than frogs. Thus they walk more than hop. Toads have no teeth, (Recall Beatrix Potter's Mrs. Tittlemouse offering the toad, Mr. Jackson some cherry stones for dinner and he declines, "No teeth, no teeth, no teeth.")

One interesting fact is that toads and frogs both stem from the order <u>anura</u>. The toad family, <u>bufanidae</u> splits off from the frog family, <u>ranidae</u>. The family <u>bufonidae</u>, contains more than 300 species, the majority of these are toads of the genus <u>bufo</u>.

Although the biology of a toad protects it from being eaten, it has no protection against pollution and the changes that global warming bring. All amphibians are very vulnerable to these assaults and could become extinct.

And About TOADS

Once upon a time, a long time ago the author was on a sailing vacation near Bayfield, Wisconsin. On those warm summer evenings when she went ashore she found the cold drink machine covered with insects attracted to the light. Sitting a foot in front of the machine was the largest toad she had ever seen. Every evening during her vacation she would again find the toad, sitting patiently, looking up toward the light and lunch! She and the toad were on friendly terms and she would pluck a mayfly or other bug as a gift to the toad who consumed it immediately, though neglecting any show of gratitude. During the day the toad was nowhere to be seen. She looked but never found him.

After the vacation was over, she continued to be curious about the daytime whereabouts of her warty skinned friend. Her musings led to the writing of the poem, TOADS. Years later she would find an artist whose watercolors captured the wonder in those summer evenings, long ago.